The Septic Bucket List

22 Things NOT to do Before You Die

I0167519

ryn gargulinski

DEDICATION

This book is dedicated to my dad, Greg Gargulinski, as it was originally created as a Christmas gift for him in 2015. Little did we know that would be his last Christmas with us. We miss him muchly but are at least glad to note he was able to avoid every single entry on this list prior to his July 2016 death.

We Love You, Dad!

And we bet there are no outhouses or cockroaches in heaven.

ACKNOWLEDGMENTS

Special thanks to my parents Greg and Marcy Gargulinski for helping me come up with this idea for a book (although Dad may have thought twice about contributing to the idea if he knew he'd be getting the book as a Christmas gift).

What the heck is a Septic Bucket List?

With all the hoopla surrounding them, you're certainly familiar with traditional bucket lists that keep track of everything you want to do before you die.

Typical entries can include things like climbing Mount Everest, eating French onion soup in France, and adopting a cat that doesn't pee on your rugs.

This isn't your typical bucket list.

The Septic Bucket List is instead exactly the opposite of the traditional list. Rather than making a lovely list of things you want to do before you die, a Septic Bucket List provides a list of things you want to avoid.

And no, none of the stuff came from first-hand experience (except maybe the construction barrel, the Brooklyn apartment, and the shoes).

Enjoy!

22 Things NOT to do Before You Die

chew through an
electric cord

get stuck
in an air duct

hand-feed raw
hamburger
to an alligator

COCKROACH FREE-FOR-ALL

RYN...

rent an apartment
above a
Brooklyn pizzeria

pick a dentist
who won't use
novocaine

handcuff yourself
to a dolphin

stick a fork
in your eye

drop your glasses
in an outhouse

swaddle yourself
in pink insulation

skinny-dip in the
Detroit River

adopt a rabid rabbit

trust sardines from
the dollar store

kick a construction
barrel while
riding your bike

attempt to bathe
a feral cat

Lick a frozen
flagpole

play hopscotch
on ice

park your car
in a pack rat zone

choose the wrong
hiking toilet paper

massage a porcupine

climb a saguaro
cactus

shoot a saguaro
cactus

shove your size 8
feet into
size 4 shoes
(even if the shoes are red
and on sale)

Live your life
Avoiding these things
And you'll have
a happy life that makes
your heart sing
- or at least a happier life than
you would if you woke up
each morn and stuck a fork
in your eye.

- Fin -

ABOUT THE AUTHOR/iLLUSTRATOR

Ryn Gargulinski is a writer, artist and performer whose journalism career began in 1991. Armed with a BFA in creative writing, an MA in English literature and a thesis in NYC subway folklore, she has written thousands of articles for newspapers and the online crowd. Credits also include writing and poetry awards, several illustrated humor books, and a Rynski art shop at rynski.etsy.com. More about Ryndustries at www.ryngargulinski.com

www.ingramcontent.com/pod-product-compliance
Lightning Source LLC
LaVergne TN
LVHW072133070426
835513LV00002B/85